RAILWAYS IN YORKSHIRE

1. West Riding

compiled by David Joy

DALESMAN BOOKS

1979

The Dalesman Publishing Company Ltd.
Clapham (via Lancaster), North Yorkshire

First published 1976

Second edition 1979

© Text 1976, 1979, David Joy

ISBN: 0 85206 494 2

Printed in Great Britain by
Galava Printing Co. Ltd., Hallam Road, Nelson, Lancashire

Contents

The cover photographs by Eric Treacy show: Front: Sowerby Bridge station with "Jubilee" No. 45717 **Dauntless** heading a Liverpool - York express; Back: The up "Thames - Clyde Express" passing through Skipton behind "Patriot" No. 45530 **Sir Frank Ree** — in the background is the now demolished original station.

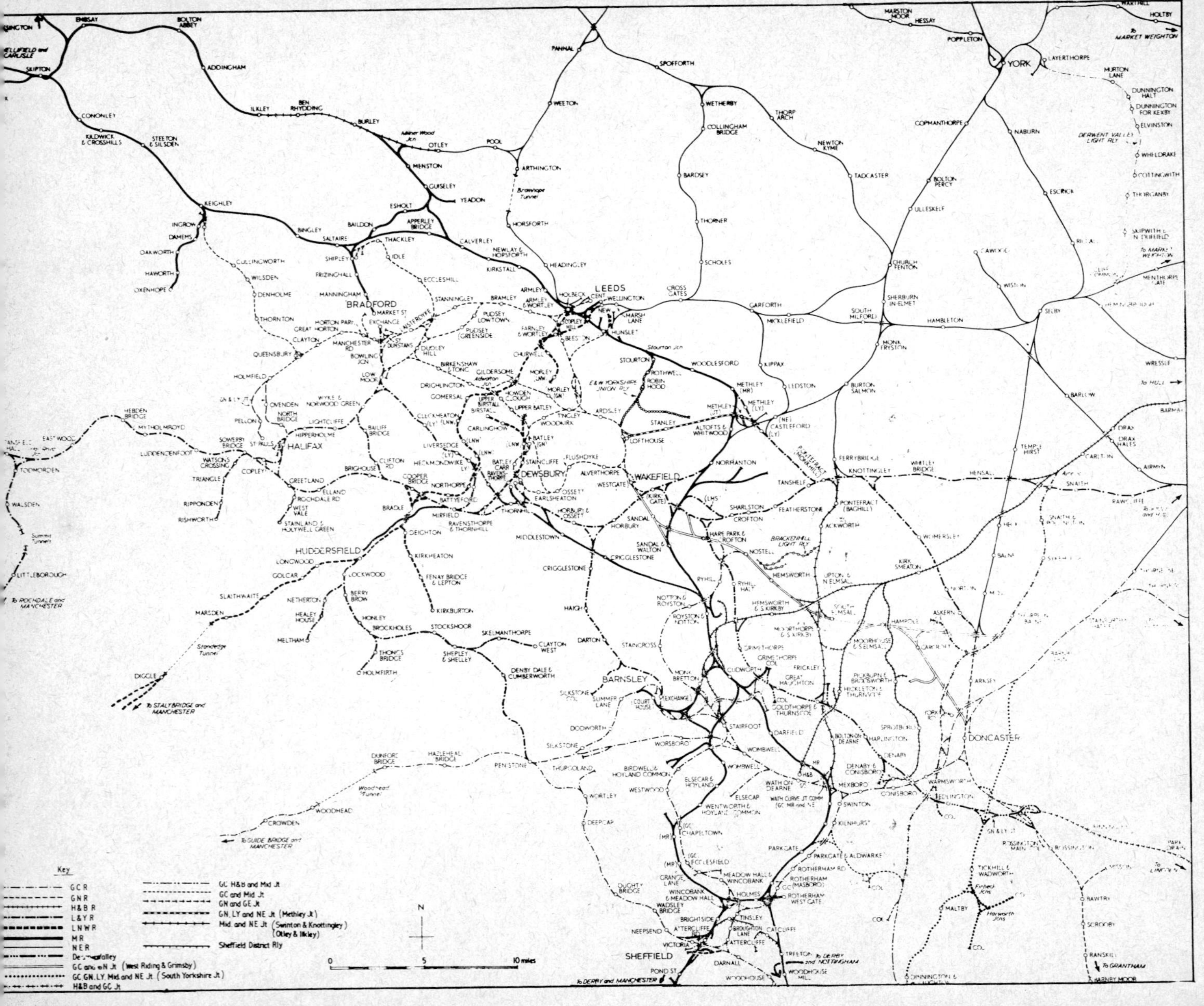

Key

GCR
GNR
H&B R
L&Y R
LNWR
MR
NER
Dearne Valley
GC and GN Jt (West Riding & Grimsby)
GC, GN, LY, Mid and NE Jt (South Yorkshire Jt)
H&B and GC Jt

GC H&B and Mid Jt
GC and Mid Jt
GN and GE Jt
GN, LY and NE Jt (Methley Jt)
Mid. and NE Jt (Swinton & Knottingley)
(Otley & Ilkley)
Sheffield District Rly

0   5   10 miles

N

YORK
LEEDS
BRADFORD
HALIFAX
HUDDERSFIELD
WAKEFIELD
DEWSBURY
BARNSLEY
DONCASTER
SHEFFIELD
ROTHERHAM

WAPLILL
HOLTBY
MARSTON MOOR
HESSAY
POPPLETON
LAYERTHORPE
MURTON LANE
DUNNINGTON HALT
DUNNINGTON FOR KEXBY
ELVINGTON
DERWENT VALLEY LIGHT RLY
WHELDRAKE
COTTINGWITH
THORGANBY
SKIPWITH & N. DUFFIELD
MENTHORPE GATE
To MARKET WEIGHTON
WRESSLE
To HULL
BARLBY
DRAX HALES
CARLTON
AIRMYN
SNAITH
RAWCLIFFE

EMBSAY
BOLTON ABBEY
ADDINGHAM
ILKLEY
BEN RHYDDING
BURLEY
OTLEY
POOL
MENSTON
GUISELEY
YEADON
ESHOLT
BALDON
APPERLEY BRIDGE
CALVERLEY
NEWLAY & HORSFORTH
HORSFORTH
HEADINGLEY
ARTHINGTON
Bramhope Tunnel
PANNAL
SPOFFORTH
WETHERBY
THORP ARCH
COLLINGHAM BRIDGE
NEWTON KYME
BARDSEY
THORNER
TADCASTER
BOLTON PERCY
COPMANTHORPE
NABURN
ULLESKELF
ESCRICK
CHURCH FENTON
SHERBURN IN ELMET
SOUTH MILFORD
HAMBLETON
SELBY
MONK FRYSTON
BURTON SALMON
LEDSTON
KIPPAX
GARFORTH
MICKLEFIELD
CROSS GATES
SCHOLES
CAWOOD
RICCALL

SKIPTON
CONONLEY
KILDWICK & CROSSHILLS
STEETON & SILSDEN
KEIGHLEY
INGROW
DAMEMS
OAKWORTH
HAWORTH
OXENHOPE
BINGLEY
SALTAIRE
SHIPLEY
IDLE
THACKLEY
ECCLESHILL
FRIZINGHALL
MANNINGHAM
CULLINGWORTH
WILSDEN
DENHOLME
THORNTON
GREAT HORTON
CLAYTON
QUEENSBURY
HOLMFIELD
HORTON PARK
MARKET ST
EXCHANGE
MANCHESTER RD
ST DUNSTANS
BOWLING JCN
LOW MOOR
DUDLEY HILL
BIRKENSHAW & TONG
GOMERSAL
DRIGHLINGTON
STANNINGLEY
BRAMLEY
LOWTOWN
PUDSEY GREENSIDE
FARNLEY & WORTLEY
ARMLEY & WORTLEY
HOLBECK
WELLINGTON
CENT.
NEW
MARSH LANE
HUNSLET
BEESTON
CHURWELL
MORLEY
STOURTON
WOODLESFORD
METHLEY
ROTHWELL
ROBIN HOOD
STANLEY
LOFTHOUSE
ARDSLEY
TINGLEY
WOODKIRK
BATLEY
UPPER BATLEY
HOWDEN CLOUGH
ADWALTON
GILDERSOME
UPPER BIRSTALL
BIRSTALL
CLECKHEATON
LIVERSEDGE
HECKMONDWIKE
CARLINGHOW
STAINCLIFFE
BATLEY CARR
SAVILLE TOWN
THORNHILL
RAVENSTHORPE & THORNHILL
MIRFIELD
DEIGHTON
NORTHORPE
COOPER BRIDGE
BATTYEFORD
BRADLEY
HORBURY & OSSET
HORBURY & OSSETT
EARLSHEATON
OSSETT
FLUSHDYKE
ALVERTHORPE
WESTGATE
WAKEFIELD (KIRK GATE)
(WESTGATE)
SANDAL & HORBURY
SANDAL & WALTON
CRIGGLESTONE
CRIGGLESTONE
HORBURY
NOSTELL
SHARLSTON
CROFTON
FEATHERSTONE
HARE PARK & CROFTON
NORMANTON
ALTOFTS & WHITWOOD
METHLEY JT
METHLEY (L.Y.)
CASTLEFORD
TYNE
FERRYBRIDGE
KNOTTINGLEY
WHITLEY BRIDGE
HENSALL
TEMPLE HIRST
PONTEFRACT (MONKHILL)
PONTEFRACT (BAGHILL)
TANSHELF
ACKWORTH
UPTON & N. ELMSALL
KIRK SMEATON
WOMERSLEY
NORTON
HAMPOLE
ASKERN
CARCROFT

HEBDEN BRIDGE
MYTHOLMROYD
EASTWOOD
TODMORDEN
WALSDEN
Summit Tunnel
LITTLEBOROUGH
To ROCHDALE and MANCHESTER
LUDDENDENFOOT
SOWERBY BRIDGE
WATSONS CROSSING
ST PAULS
TRIANGLE
COPLEY
GREETLAND
RIPPONDEN
RISHWORTH
WEST VALE
STAINLAND & HOLYWELL GREEN
ELLAND
BRIGHOUSE
CLIFTON RD
ROCHDALE RD
NORTHORPE
PELLON
NORTH BRIDGE
OVENDEN
WYKE & NORWOOD GREEN
LIGHTCLIFFE
HIPPERHOLME
BAILIFF BRIDGE
GN & LY JT
HEBDEN BRIDGE
MIDDLESTOWN
LONGWOOD
GOLCAR
SLAITHWAITE
MARSDEN
Standedge Tunnel
DIGGLE
To STALYBRIDGE and MANCHESTER
LOCKWOOD
BERRY BROW
NETHERTON
HEALEY HOUSE
HONLEY
BROCKHOLES
MELTHAM
HOLMFIRTH
THONGS BRIDGE
SHEPLEY & SHELLEY
KIRKHEATON
FENAY BRIDGE & LEPTON
KIRKBURTON
STOCKSMOOR
SKELMANTHORPE
CLAYTON WEST
DENBY DALE & CUMBERWORTH
HAIGH
DARTON
STAINCROSS
CRIGGLESTONE
RYHILL
NOTTON & ROYSTON
ROYSTON & NOTTON
RYHILL HALT
HEMSWORTH
HEMSWORTH & S. KIRKBY
NORTHORPE & S. KIRKBY
SOUTH ELMSALL
MOORHOUSE & S. ELMSALL
DUNFORD BRIDGE
HAZLEHEAD BRIDGE
PENISTONE
THURGOLAND
BIRDWELL & HOYLAND COMMON
WORTLEY
WESTWOOD
DEEPCAR
Woodhead Tunnel
WOODHEAD
CROWDEN
To GUIDE BRIDGE and MANCHESTER
DODWORTH
SILKSTONE
WORSBRO
SILKSTONE COL.
SUMMER LANE
COURT HOUSE
EXCHANGE
STAIRFOOT
DARFIELD
WOMBWELL
MONK BRETTON
CUDWORTH
GRIMETHORPE
GRIMETHORPE COL.
FRICKLEY
GREAT HOUGHTON
GOLDTHORPE & THURNSCOE
BOLTON ON DEARNE
HARLINGTON
DENABY & CONISBORO
DENABY
PICKBURN & BRODSWORTH
HICKLETON & THURNSCOE
SPROTBOROUGH
WARMSWORTH
CONISBRO
MEXBORO
SWINTON
KILNHURST
ELSECAR & HOYLAND
WENTWORTH & HOYLAND COMMON
ELSECAR
WATH ON DEARNE
WATH CURVE JT COMM (GC MR and NE)
CHAPELTOWN
ECCLESFIELD
PARKGATE
PARKGATE & ALDWARKE
ROTHERHAM RD
ROTHERHAM (MASBRO)
ROTHERHAM WEST GATE
GRANGE LANE
OUGHTY BRIDGE
MEADOW HALL & WINCOBANK
WINCOBANK & MEADOW HALL
WADSLEY BRIDGE
HOLMES
BRIGHTSIDE
NEEPSEND
ATTERCLIFFE
TINSLEY
BROUGHTON LANE
CATCLIFFE
VICTORIA
DARNALL
WOODHOUSE
WOODHOUSE MILL
SHEFFIELD
POND ST
To DERBY and MANCHESTER
TREETON
To DERBY (2nd NOTTINGHAM)
To GRANTHAM
BARNBY MOOR
RANSKILL
SCROOBY
BAWTRY
MALTBY
TICKHILL & WADWORTH
FIRBECK JCNS
HAYWORTH JCNS
KIVETON
DINNINGTON & LAUGHTON
ROSSINGTON
BLAXTON
FINNINGLEY
MISSON
To LINCOLN
BRANBY MOOR
BELLINGTON

Introduction

This book is the first of three volumes devoted to each of the Ridings of Yorkshire, an arrangement which needs no apology but does require an explanation. The historic Ridings were a regrettable casualty of local government reorganisation in 1974 when they were replaced by North, South and West Yorkshire with additional portions of the county being hived off to Lancashire, Cumbria, Durham, Cleveland and Humberside. However, not only are the boundaries of the traditional Ridings still far more familiar than those of the new counties, but they also provide a much more satisfactory division of the area's railway network. This first volume covers the railways of the West Riding — with two important exceptions. One is the famous Settle and Carlisle line which has its own volume in this series of pictorial histories: **Settle - Carlisle Centenary** compiled by David Joy & W. R. Mitchell (Dalesman Books, 1975). The other concerns the relatively few North Eastern lines in the West Riding, which more logically are included in the East and North Riding volumes given over almost entirely to this geographically monopolistic company. The overriding theme throughout the series is to present "not just a collection of views, but an attempt to portray the character and customs, the pride and prejudice and the architectural attributes and atrocities of a region's various lines in their prime. Photographs taken during different decades show how fast the scene can change, and how a feature taken for granted can almost overnight become but a memory".

The West Riding had in many ways the most complex railway network in the country. Its large population and its coal, steel and woollen riches acted as a magnet to most of the main line companies in the North which like birds of prey vied with one another to plunder the region's wealth. Ultimately two Anglo-Scottish main lines passed through the Riding in the form of the Midland and East Coast routes, and in addition two other companies — the London & North Western and the Great Central — provided direct links to the capital. This created extraordinary duplication as instanced by services from Halifax before the second world war when within the space of little over two hours one could catch through trains to four different London termini — King's Cross, Euston, St. Pancras and Marylebone! Again, there was a multiplicity of trans-Pennine routes with two from Manchester to Leeds and two from Manchester to Sheffield (one of these was the Midland's Hope Valley line which will be covered in the Derbyshire volume in this series). The same pattern continued eastwards with the Great Central, North Eastern and Hull & Barnsley companies all at one time operating services between Sheffield and Hull. Even with long-distance traffic a passenger could often choose between rival companies for through trains, for example from Leeds to Edinburgh, Bradford to Bournemouth or Sheffield to Llandudno. Less spectacular but far more important financially was the competition for freight and mineral traffic, in particular for coal from South Yorkshire to Lancashire and the

Humber ports and for woollen goods from the northern half of the West Riding. The Grouping of 1923 ended neither the competition nor the duplication as lines belonging to the six major companies in the area were fairly evenly divided between the LMS and the LNER (the former absorbed the Midland, London & North Western and Lancashire & Yorkshire, and the latter the Great Northern, Great Central and Hull & Barnsley). It was left to nationalisation and finally the Beeching Plan to bring about a long overdue weeding out of surplus lines and stations.

The traditional image of the West Riding as a continuous sprawl of mill chimneys and pit-head winding gear dies hard, and even in the heyday of heavy industry many parts of the region were unblemished stretches of rolling and wooded countryside. Yet the grand scale of both the topography and the man-made landscape tended to lessen the impact of the railways' engineering works which throughout the area were often monumental in concept and stupendous in execution. The successful challenging of harsh contours meant that more than 30 route miles of line were in tunnels, with some continuous bores of over three miles in length through the Pennine watershed and other tunnels in excess of a mile at Morley, Queensbury and Gildersome. Fully visible and hence even more spectacular were the many mighty viaducts, varying from the 34 arches of Lockwood, near Huddersfield, towering 136 feet above the river Holme, to the long and low 99 arches at Wakefield which consumed 800 million bricks in striding across the Calder for nearly three-quarters of a mile. In addition to these impressive statistics, a cutting at Chevet on the Midland main line south of Wakefield and an embankment on the Great Northern's Pudsey loop were respectively claimed as the deepest and highest in the country.

Assembling a representative photographic portrayal of West Riding railways has proved exceptionally difficult. Until comparatively recent times most photographers seldom seemed to venture west of Doncaster, perhaps being deterred by the smoke haze which so frequently blanketed the region. Even when they did make venturesome forays into the interior, the pioneers almost invariably concentrated on the more glamorous passenger trains and ignored the freight services which formed the area's lifeblood. This collection has in fact slowly been built up over a period of almost ten years, and as can be seen from the acknowledgements on page 80 has come from many sources. Every effort has been made to trace copyright holders, but apologies are tendered in the case of any infringements which may inadvertently have occurred.

This book is subdivided into sections broadly devoted to lines built by each of the dominant pre-Grouping companies in the area, with a final section given over to the Hull & Barnsley and the joint mineral lines in South Yorkshire. In each case historical notes give a concise summary of development, but for fuller information one should refer to the following selected list of further reading:

Baughan, Peter E., **North of Leeds: The Leeds - Settle - Carlisle Line and its Branches** (Roundhouse, 1966).

Baughan, Peter E., **The Railways of Wharfedale** (David & Charles, 1969).

Binns, Donald, **The Railways of Craven** (Hendon, 1974).

Dow, George, **Great Central** (Locomotive Publishing Co., 3 vols., 1959-65).

Dunstan, John, **The Origins of the Sheffield and Chesterfield Railway** (Dore Village Society, 1970).

Elliott, B. J., **The South Yorkshire Joint Railway** (Oakwood Press, 1972).

Franks, D. L., **East and West Yorkshire Union Railways** (Turntable Publications, 1973).

Franks, D. L., **South Yorkshire Railway** (Turntable Publications, 1971).

Goode, C. T., **Railways in South Yorkshire** (Dalesman Books, 1975).

Grinling, Charles H., **The History of the Great Northern Railway** (new edition, Allen & Unwin, 1966).

Haigh, A., **Railways in West Yorkshire** (Dalesman Books, 1974).

Hoole, K. (edit.), **The Hull & Barnsley Railway, Vol. 1** (David & Charles, 1972).

Joy, David, **A Regional History of the Railways of Great Britain: Vol. 8: South and West Yorkshire** (David & Charles, 1975).

Lambert, Richard S., **The Railway King 1800-1871: A Study of George Hudson and the business morals of his time** (Allen & Unwin, 2nd impression, 1964).

Marshall, John, **The Lancashire & Yorkshire Railway** (David & Charles, 3 vols., 1969-72).

Nock, O. S., **The London & North Western Railway** (Ian Allan, 1960).

Povey, R. O. T., **The History of the Keighley & Worth Valley Railway** (Keighley & Worth Valley Railway Preservation Society, 2nd edit., 1968).

Sheffield City Libraries, **A Railway Chronology of the Sheffield Area** (2nd edit., 1961).

Stocks, William B., **Pennine Journey: The History of the Railways, Tramways and Canals in Huddersfield and District** (Advertiser Press, 1958).

Williams, Frederick S., **The Midland Railway: Its Rise and Progress** (new impression, David & Charles, 1969).

Midland Memories

The Midland main line was the only trunk route passing through the West Riding for a really substantial distance, entering the region through the foothills of the Peak District and leaving it far to the north-west on the summit reaches of the Settle & Carlisle line. It had its origins in 1840 when the opening of the North Midland Railway completed a chain of lines stretching from London (Euston Square) to Leeds — the equivalent of the present day M1 motorway. The North Midland was engineered by George Stephenson, the "Father of Railways", who attached paramount importance to keeping gradients to an absolute minimum. In this case he perhaps carried the concept too far, so that the line clung tenaciously to the river valleys and created enormous dissent by brushing Sheffield, Barnsley and Wakefield to one side. From Chesterfield it penetrated the West Riding via Killamarsh and Rotherham before reaching the key early railway junction of Normanton, once described as "the Crewe of the coalfields". Here the Manchester & Leeds Railway trailed in from the west (see page 54), while George Hudson's York & North Midland Railway diverged to the north-east. Until the opening of the upstart Great Northern line in 1850, the established East Coast Route to York, Newcastle and Scotland was via Derby and Normanton.

By 1850 Hudson had been toppled from his throne as "the railway king", but six years earlier he had brought about the first major railway amalgamation when he merged the North Midland with two other companies centred on Derby. The combined system was known simply as the Midland Railway, which became one of the most colourful, impressive and popular of the pre-Grouping lines.

It gradually transformed itself from a provincial company to an Anglo-Scottish trunk route by a series of "take-overs" which took it north-west from Leeds firstly to Bradford, Skipton and Colne, and then to Lancaster and Morecambe. An offshoot of this line made an end-on junction at Ingleton with the Midland's great rival, the London & North Western Railway, giving a direct but highly unsatisfactory link to Carlisle and Scotland. Years of frustration over deliberately bad connections finally drove the Midland to complete its magnificent Settle & Carlisle line over the roof of the Pennines, opened in 1876. In the meantime the company had either built or acquired West Riding branches to Barnsley, Oxenhope, Barnoldswick and, jointly with the North Eastern Railway, Otley and Ilkley. Most important of all, it had placed Sheffield on a direct route to the south, opening a new loop via Dore & Totley which was followed by virtually all passenger traffic.

The Midland with its longer and more mountainous main line was never able to compete with the East and West Coast Routes in terms of speed, but made up for this by its superbly comfortable rolling stock and the scenic delights on the journey. It began to slip into decline as an Anglo-Scottish route soon after the Grouping in 1923, and today is traversed throughout by just one daytime and one night-time express. Inter-City traffic is still substantial south of Leeds, but of the many fascinating West Riding branches only that to Ilkley remains open for regular traffic. The Worth Valley line to Haworth and Oxenhope has however found a new lease of life under the auspices of a preservation society and happily caters for enthusiasts of both steam and the Brontës.

Dore & Totley, the Midland gateway to Yorkshire following the completion in 1870 of the company's "Sheffield loop" which is on the right of this photograph. The train on the left is on the newer line to Chinley and Manchester, opened in 1894 and passing through the 3 miles 950 yards Totley tunnel. The date of this view is about 1905.

A fine period study of
the façade of
Sheffield Midland
station before its
rebuilding in 1900-5.
These buildings are
now on one of the
island platforms.

The rebuilt Sheffield Midland station in pre-Grouping days with Johnson 2-4-0 No. 266 pausing at the platform face.

Sheffield Midland grew into something of an architectural hotch-potch. Part of the station had an overall roof as shown in this 1936 view of class 5MT 4-6-0 No. 5183 on a Bradford (Forster Square) - St. Pancras express.

A remarkable view of Sheffield (Wicker) goods yard about 1923.
The volume and variety of traffic seems almost incredible by present day
standards, while the horse drays and lamps are of particular note.
Wicker was the Sheffield terminus of the early Sheffield & Rotherham
Railway, opened in 1838.

The North Midland Railway, extending from Derby to Leeds, was one of the early trunk main lines laid out in the grand manner by George Stephenson. It was opened in 1840 at a time when railway companies could afford the luxury of commissioning leading architects — in this case Francis Thompson — to design stations on an individual basis. The elegant proportions of one such station, Swinton, in the then rural Don valley, are shown in this lithograph by S. Russell.

The same station in 1899, when both the building and its surroundings had become distinctly tarnished. It is about to be replaced by a more utilitarian structure, just visible in the background.

Coal on the move — one of the commonest yet least photographed railway scenes in the West Riding. 0-6-0 No. 612 is passing through Cudworth on the Midland main line in 1900.

Cudworth was the junction for a short Midland branch to Barnsley (Court House), opened in 1870 and closed in 1958. Johnson 0-4-4T No. 58075 is at work on the branch push-and-pull service at Barnsley in early British Railways days.

A major improvement on the Midland main line took place in 1923-5 when the 684 yards Chevet tunnel, between Cudworth and Normanton, was opened out to create what at almost 100 feet was claimed to be the deepest railway cutting in the country. Note the contractor's locomotive on the left in this view of the south portal.

Normanton, now a ghost station but once ''the Crewe of the coalfields'' and the most important early railway junction in the West Riding. Later it became the refreshment stop for Anglo-Scottish expresses before the introduction of dining cars. The covered footbridge leading direct from the platforms to the station hotel is a noteworthy survival.

Immaculately groomed Johnson 0-4-4T No. 1546 sports express headlamps as it prepares to work a train from the south forward from Leeds (Wellington) to Bradford (Forster Square). In the background is Leeds (New), now the only passenger station for services to and from Leeds.

Leeds (Wellington) in
Midland days. The terminus
was drastically rebuilt in 1938
when it was combined with
Leeds (New) to form Leeds
(City). The present Queen's
Hotel was erected at the
same time.

A 1933 study of 2-4-0 No. 242
backing on to the Bradford
portion of an ex-London
express at Leeds
(Wellington). This member of
the class has been rebuilt
with a Belpaire firebox.

The original Bradford (Market Street) station before its replacement in 1890 by the present Forster Square Terminus. Hansom cabs queue up for business, and posters advertise the delights of such varied destinations as Worcester and New York !

Bradford (Forster Square) about 1910, with two recently arrived expresses on the right. Today only two platforms of this station are in passenger use for services to Keighley and Ilkley.

Saltaire station, opened in 1859 to serve Titus Salt's "palace of industry" —a ten acre alpaca and mohair mill, part of which is visible in the background.

Damems on the Worth Valley branch from Keighley to Oxenhope was claimed to be the smallest station on the Midland Railway. Even so, it was complete down to the last detail with ground frame, posters, water butt, fire buckets, porter's barrow, lamp and station dog. Although a farmer once reputedly took the station away in mistake for a hen hut, it still survives on the preserved Worth Valley Railway.

Oxenhope, terminus of the Worth Valley branch, is shown here about 1905 when it had four station staff. The buildings remain basically unaltered to the present day.

By contrast, Grassington & Threshfield — terminus of the Yorkshire Dales Railway from Embsay — has vanished in the wake of a housing estate. This view shows the jubilant opening festivities in 1902, but regular passenger services ended as early as 1930.

The Ilkley - Skipton line was mainly traversed by local services prior to its demise in 1965, but occasionally rose to greater heights. Here "Patriot" 4-6-0 No. 45505 **The Royal Army Ordnance Corps** is leaving Ilkley with a return excursion to Whaley Bridge, near Stockport, in 1955.

Skipton station in the LMS period. The main running lines are on the left, and in the centre is the down platform loop normally used by local services from Bradford and to Lancashire. The Ilkley lines are on the right.

Unusual motive power at Skipton in 1956 in the form of Stanier "Pacific" No. 46225 **Duchess of Gloucester** undergoing dynometer car trials between Shipley and Carlisle.

Bustle at Gargrave as a Johnson 2-4-0 pauses on a down stopping train. The varied rolling stock includes some clerestory-roofed coaches at the rear of the train.

The Midland line from Skipton to Colne penetrated into Lancashire, but before doing so threw off a short branch for Barnoldswick at Earby. Here Kirtley 0-6-0 No. 2404 heads the quite respectable-looking branch train at Earby.

Johnson 0-4-4T No. 1357, still in LMS livery, on the one-coach branch train at Barnoldswick in August 1948. The line was built by the independent Barnoldswick Railway and later taken over by the Midland; it was closed in 1966.

Prior to the opening of the Settle - Carlisle railway in 1876, Midland traffic reached Scotland by reluctant courtesy of the London & North Western Railway. The two companies met at Ingleton, each having separate stations at either end of the viaduct which acted as a sort of no man's land. This view probably dates from the 1860s and shows a London & North Western engine and train on the viaduct.

Great Northern Echoes

The Great Northern was a latecomer among trunk main lines. Sanctioned at the height of the "railway mania" in 1846, it was a deliberate and concerted attempt to break George Hudson's stranglehold of the East Coast Route by building a direct main line from London to York via Peterborough, Grantham and Doncaster. Thirty miles shorter than Hudson's route through Derby and Normanton, the Great Northern obviously attracted the full wrath of the "railway king" who denounced it as "the most complete monopoly ever sought to be established". Yet all his efforts failed to prevent Parliament giving its blessing to the largest ever single railway scheme in terms of both mileage and capital. Hudson's kingdom was split asunder, and he disappeared from the scene in 1849, a year before Great Northern trains commenced running north from London. The company never reached York in its own right, but in the classic utterance of its first chairman "terminated in a ploughed field four miles north of Doncaster" from where it relied on running powers over other lines. Nevertheless the Great Northern immediately formed the accepted southern portion of the shortened East Coast Route, and at the same time revolutionised aristocratic Doncaster by choosing the town for the site of its locomotive works.

Yet somehow both Doncaster and the associated portion of the new East Coast main line seemed to have stronger affinities with Lincolnshire than with the real West Riding. It was west of Wakefield that Great Northern lines were at one with the local terrain, although curiously the company did not have exclusive access to the county town from the south and again depended initially on running powers. Only when it had absorbed a considerable network of lines beyond Wakefield did it manage to acquire a new route from Doncaster jointly with the Manchester, Sheffield & Lincolnshire Railway. The most important portion of this network extended to Leeds (Central) and then on to Bradford (Exchange), although there were other more steeply graded approaches to the West Riding's wool capital via the breezy heights of Morley or through Dewsbury and Batley. Other lines included the Methley Joint linking Lofthouse and Castleford, the Pudsey loop and the outer suburban route from Laisterdyke to Shipley through Eccleshill and Idle. Finally there were the amazing Queensbury lines, a hopelessly unrealistic attempt by the Great Northern to compete with older established routes from Bradford to Halifax and Keighley.

The West Riding was fortunate at the Grouping in that the Great Northern became part of the LNER and the Midland a constituent of the LMS, so that services from both Leeds and Bradford remained competitive. The LNER'S most publicised passenger development in this region was the introduction in 1937 of the high-speed "West Riding Limited" hauled by Gresley's streamlined A4s. It comes as something of a shock to realise that almost forty years ago home-produced energy was whisking passengers up from Leeds to London in a time only minutes slower than that achieved by today's diesels. In fact the ex Great Northern lines in the area suffer particularly badly in present day comparisons for the simple reason that most of them have ceased to exist. Of the once substantial network, only the basic main line from Doncaster to Bradford via Leeds still carries passenger traffic.

The Great Northern Railway entered the West Riding near Rossington, south of Doncaster Here "Atlantic" No. 282 is passing through the station with a King's Cross - Harrogate express composed of a most motley collection of rolling stock.

Doncaster station, prior to its rebuilding in the late 1930s when the pillars between the running lines were removed and the roofs cut back.

Strange partners in the shape of ex Great Northern "Atlantic" No. 3254 and ex Great Central 4-6-0 No. 5424 **City of Lincoln** leaving Doncaster on the York - Harwich boat train. A rake of articulated coaches is in the background.

The famous "Plant" locomotive works were established at Doncaster in 1853, and eventually covered 200 acres and employed 4,500 men. This 1938 view shows A4s Nos. 4500 **Sir Ronald Matthews** (left) and 2510 **Quicksilver** in the repair shop.

A bird's eye view of Doncaster sheds in 1932 with many different locomotive classes in evidence.
A stranger in the camp is LMS 0-6-0 No. 12120 in the foreground.

The flat lands or "carrs" around Doncaster are prone to severe flooding from time to time. A particularly bad bout occurred in 1932 when the river Don was over two miles wide and long stretches of the East Coast main line were washed out. Here the "Flying Scotsman", headed by A3 No. 2596 **Manna**, is flagged past repaired track near Arksey as a permanent way train stands just clear of the water in a siding.

Curious architecture on the West Riding & Grimsby Joint Railway which gave the Great Northern access from Doncaster to its many lines west of Wakefield. Carcroft & Adwick-le-Street, opened in 1866, contains chapel, cottage and station elements in its design.

Wakefield (Westgate), equally distinctive in its way with an Italianate clock tower extending to 97 feet above street level. N1 0-6-2T No. 69464 is heading the Bradford portion of a London express.

More distinctive architecture as seen at Stanley on the Methley Joint Railway, over which the Great Northern worked a Leeds - Castleford service. The other partners in this line, which closed in 1964, were the Lancashire & Yorkshire and North Eastern railways.

Dudley Hill station on the Bradford - Wakefield line with its remarkable hexagonal booking hall topped by a louvred lantern and weather vane ! This probably dates from 1893 when the station became the junction for a short-lived line to Low Moor.

One of the **distinc**tive Great Northern rail **mot**ors which provided a shuttle service between Ossett and Chickenley Heath until tramcar competition caused its withdrawal in 1909. Like many.such services it gained a nickname — in this case "the Chickenley Coddy".

Dewsbury (Central), a typical Great Northern island platform station, with ex Great Central 4-4-2T No. 7444 heading a Wakefield - Leeds via Batley local in 1948. The station gained its greatest glory in 1954 when it had a royal visit and was repainted — on one side only !

Proud moment at Leeds (Central) on September 23rd, 1937, with streamlined A4 No. 4495 **Golden Fleece** about to depart on a demonstration run of the new "West Riding Limited" express. The outbreak of war in 1939 caused the demise of this high-speed service scheduled to run up to London in 2 hours 44 minutes, only 12 minutes slower than the fastest of today's diesel powered services.

Two named trains at Leeds (Central). A4 No. 60015 **Quicksilver** is about to depart with the up "White Rose", while on the left the "Queen of Scots Pullman" has arrived from London and will continue to Glasgow after reversal. J50 0-6-0T No. 68988 is on station pilot duties, and on the right is one of the diesel units introduced on Bradford services as early as 1954. Leeds (Central) closed in 1967 and all services were transferred to Leeds (City).

Above: The original Laisterdyke station in 1870 with a remarkable assemblage of station staff and passengers. Note the station horse on the extreme left shunting wagons presumably containing bales of wool.
Right: A forgotten but nevertheless imposing terminus was Bradford (Adolphus Street), closed to passengers as early as 1867 when Great Northern services were transferred to Bradford (Exchange).

Something like half a century separates these two views of the handsome Great Northern 4-4-2 tanks at work in the West Riding. This pre-Grouping study shows No. 1020 carefully groomed for station pilot duties at Bradford (Exchange).

In BR days No. 67372 heads a Leeds - Bradford local through Holbeck (High Level) prior to the introduction of diesel units in 1954. This station was used almost entirely for interchange purposes with Holbeck (Low Level) immediately below.

The many Great Northern branches in the Bradford area included the Pudsey loop, closed in 1964. A typical suburban train of the pre-diesel age, hauled by N1 0-6-2T No. 69477, has halted alongside a characteristic Great Northern "somersault" signal at Pudsey Greenside.

A lesser known branch was the outer suburban line from Laisterdyke to Shipley via Eccleshill, Idle and Thackley which lost its passenger services as early as 1931. This rare photograph, one of the few known views of a passenger train on the line, shows 4-4-2T No. 4549 at the Shipley & Windhill terminus.

The Queensbury lines linking Bradford, Halifax and Keighley were among the most spectacularly engineered and least profitable in the West Riding. Yet the stations were built on the grand scale as is shown by this view of Great Horton between Bradford and Queensbury. N1 0-6-2T No. 69442, fitted with condensing gear for working underground lines in the London area, is hauling a two-coach train.

An early view of the unique Queensbury station with continuous platforms on three sides of a triangular junction. Those on the Bradford - Keighley line in the background were tiered out from the viaduct, while the triangle was pierced by a colliery waggonway. Originally there was a signal box at each point of the triangle. The station, more than a mile in distance and 400 feet in altitude from the township it purported to serve, was an early casualty of tramcar competition.

At Holmfield the Queensbury lines linked up with the Halifax High Level Railway, built as the name suggests to serve the high-lying western edge of the town and terminating at St. Paul's some 325 feet above the level of the main station. This view of a Great Northern saddle tank near the intermediate station of Pellon is of considerable interest as passenger services lasted only from 1890 to 1917.

Another Great Northern saddle tank is hauling a surprisingly heavy freight across Hewenden viaduct, between Wilsden and Cullingworth, at just over 900 feet the highest point on both the Queensbury lines and the Great Northern Railway. Although now trackless, it still survives as an impressive monument to an age of reckless enterprise.

The last day of passenger services on the Queensbury lines — May 21st. 1955. An N1 0-6-2T pauses at Wilsden on a Bradford - Keighley train, a service which from the outset was unable to compete with the shorter Midland route via Shipley.

Rails to Huddersfield

Of the three main lines which crossed the Pennines from Manchester to the West Riding, the most grandiose was that of the London & North Western Railway. Its tunnels through the watershed at Standedge seemed to set the tone and standards of the whole route. The initial single line tunnel of 3 miles 66 yards in length was the longest in Britain for nearly forty years from its opening in 1849 until the completion of the Severn tunnel in 1886. Eventually it was joined by an additional single line and a double line tunnel, the parallel bores containing unique "underground" water troughs as they formed the only suitable level stretch on this steeply graded route. Then the four tracks descended the Colne Valley in impressive style to Huddersfield station with its magnificent façade forming the only railway architecture of any real merit in the whole of the West Riding. Over 400 feet long and boasting a central portico 68 feet high, the laying of its foundation stone was a matter of such pride that a holiday was declared and the church bells rang from dawn to dusk.

North-east from Huddersfield, the London & North Western found it impossible to quadruple its original main line to Leeds which shared tracks with the Lancashire & Yorkshire at Mirfield and then passed through Dewsbury and the 1 mile 1,609 yards Morley tunnel. So at the turn of the century it built the Leeds New Line, cutting out all conflicting junctions, attracting additional traffic from the Spen Valley towns and gaining another major West Riding tunnel in the 1 mile 571 yards bore at Gildersome. These lines represented the London & North Western's only major incursion into the West Riding, but were characteristic of a company which with total lack of modesty styled itself the "Premier Line" and boasted that it was "noted for Punctuality, Speed, Smooth Riding, Dustless Tracks, Safety and Comfort".

The other railways running into Huddersfield should logically have formed part of the London & North Western empire, but instead became an isolated portion of the Lancashire & Yorkshire system during the cut-and-thrust politics of the "railway mania". The basic link ran south to Penistone through most attractive countryside, cutting across several river valleys by a succession of viaducts and tunnels. Apart from local services it was used by expresses to Sheffield, some of which worked forward to London –– at first to King's Cross and then later to Marylebone. Diverging from this cross-country route were some of the most attractive branch lines in the West Riding, running along tributary valleys to serve the small townships of Meltham, Holmfirth and Clayton West. This last branch still survives, existing like the Huddersfield - Penistone line as a whole on borrowed time for as long ago as 1881 its working costs exceeded receipts.

The picture on the main line through Huddersfield is somewhat happier for it is now the only one of the three trans-Pennine routes still carrying passenger services throughout. Even so there has been talk of concentrating all traffic on the Calder Valley route which would make Huddersfield the largest West Riding settlement to be deprived of its rail facilities. The Leeds New Line has already succumbed, the last trains running over it in 1966, and substantial stretches have now been obliterated by new housing estates.

The London & North Western entered the West Riding in fine style with a four track main line running down the Colne Valley from Standedge tunnel to Huddersfield. The local scenery is well shown in this study of a class 5MT 4-6-0 storming up the climb to Standedge near Marsden.

Described by John Betjeman as "the most splendid station facade in England", Huddersfield is the only railway building of any real distinction in the whole of the West Riding. The station buildings were purchased by Huddersfield Corporation to mark the centenary of the Borough in 1968, and have been splendidly restored.

After the magnificent frontage, the interior of Huddersfield station comes as something of an anti-climax. This long train stretching away into the distance is a Blackpool excursion in about 1925.

Two companies at Huddersfield about 1922. On the left is a London & North Western "Claughton" on a Liverpool express, and on the right is a Great Central 0-6-2T on one of the daily freights from Penistone.

Ex London & North Western "coal tank" No. 7722 poses for the camera during a break in station pilot duties at Huddersfield.

The grandeur of a double-headed London & North Western express. "Experiment" class 4-6-0 No. 165 **City of Lichfield** pilots a "Claughton" 4-6-0 into Huddersfield.

Quadrupling the London & North Western main line from Huddersfield to Leeds would have been prohibitively expensive, so instead the company built a long loop in the form of the ''Leeds New Line'' which at the same time served several textile towns in the Spen Valley. This view shows an impressive array of overbridges at Heckmondwike, photographed shortly after completion of the line in 1900.

The major engineering work on the ''Leeds New Line'' was the 1 mile 571 yards Gildersome tunnel, seen here in the 1930s with a ''Prince of Wales'' 4-6-0 emerging into daylight. Passenger services were withdrawn from this route in 1965, and much of the area round the tunnel has been transformed by the M62 motorway.

The Huddersfield - Penistone
line and its associated
branches were owned by the
Lancashire & Yorkshire
Railway, but were physically
separated from the other
metals of that company.
This secondary route cut
across the grain of the
country, the finest of its many
engineering works being the
136 feet high Lockwood
viaduct — with its 34 arches
one of the longest in the
country.

An interesting group of
station staff and passengers
at Thongs Bridge on the
Holmfirth branch, opened in
1850 and closed to
passengers in 1959. Like most
Lancashire & Yorkshire
branches, it had the luxury of
double track.

One of the many tunnels on the Huddersfield - Penistone line was that at Lockwood, seen in the 1930s with 0-6-0 No. 13231 emerging. Note the water tower hard against the tunnel portal.

Perhaps the most famous feature of the Huddersfield - Penistone line was this carving at Berry Brow station. It was executed in 1886 by J. C. Stocks and depicts a Barton Wright 0-4-4T and train surmounted by a facial study of Thomas Swinburn who was an engineer on the line.
The carving was moved to York Railway Museum in 1963.

Timber trestles are **more** associated with the **Canadian** Rockies than the West Riding with its abundance of stone. Yet a number were built, one of the largest being this structure at Denby Dale which terrified timid passengers owing to the way the timber shook when trains crossed. Eventually it was declared unsafe, and is seen here being dismantled in 1884 following completion of the adjacent stone viaduct.

Among the attractive branch termini in the Huddersfield area was Meltham, end of a $3\frac{1}{2}$ mile branch from Lockwood which was opened to passengers in 1869 and closed in 1949. Like most of the branches in this area, it passed through pleasant rural surroundings for much of its length.

Holmfirth was another spacious and generously laid out terminus. At one time there were plans to extend the line up the valley to Holmbridge but these never materialised.

The London & North Western main line entered Leeds on a long and curving viaduct taking it over much of Holbeck. This 1958 view shows Holbeck sheds in the foreground, the Midland main line on the right, and the London & North Western viaduct in the background. Crossing it is a Newcastle - Liverpool express double-headed by an unrebuilt and rebuilt "Patriot".

The London & North Western shared Leeds (New) station with the North Eastern Railway. On January 13th, 1892, a disaster occurred when a destructive fire broke out in a tallow works situated in the "Dark Arches" beneath the station. It lasted for two days, and caused disruption of traffic for several weeks.

A familiar scene at Leeds (City), formerly Leeds (New), until the 1960s was that of Newcastle - Liverpool expresses changing engines. Often an A3 "Pacific" would give way to a pair of ex LMS locomotives for the stiff climb over the Pennines. This evocative photograph shows "Jubilee" No. 45709 and unrebuilt "Scott" No. 46137 awaiting departure for the west in December 1952.

London & North Western engines on unfamiliar metals. Nos. 117 "Alaska" and 1709 "Princess Mary" depart from Collingham Bridge on July 8th, 1908, with the royal train conveying King Edward VII from Harewood House to Eaton Hall, Chester. The North Eastern Railway stand-by engine is on the right.

The Calder Valley

The earliest — and also the most indirect — of the trans-Pennine routes into the West Riding was that of the Manchester & Leeds Railway completed in 1841. Like the pioneer north - south line into the region — the North Midland Railway — it was engineered by George Stephenson, but in this case the rugged landscape forced him to abandon his cherished ideal of 1 in 330 as a maximum gradient. He did well to keep the steepest incline on the Yorkshire side of the Pennines to a reasonable 1 in 160 by tunnelling through the watershed at Summit, south of Todmorden, before following the sinuous and extremely constricted upper reaches of the Calder Valley. The line then avoided the key centres of Halifax, Huddersfield and Dewsbury but did manage to serve Wakefield prior to reaching Normanton, from where much to its chagrin the company had to share the tracks of the North Midland into Leeds. The major engineering work on the route was the 1 mile 1,125 yards tunnel at Summit, the longest in the world when it was completed at a cost of £251,000.

In 1847 the Manchester & Leeds became the Lancashire & Yorkshire Railway, for many years an appalling line which earned the description of "probably the most degenerate railway in the kingdom" owing to its disregard for punctuality and passenger comforts as well as a generally restrictive policy. Feelings ran particularly high in the West Riding. The company was the target of insult and ridicule at every opportunity, and a favourite pantomime doggerel began:

He went to Bradford for to dine
By the Lancashire and Yorkshire line,
He waited three weeks at bleak Low Moor,
And when he complained the porter swore
That he ought to have started a month before . . .

Low Moor was among the notorious junction stations on the system — others being Mirfield and Todmorden — and was on the important northern extension through Halifax to Bradford (Exchange). It was served by a feeder line from the Spen Valley, giving a direct link between Bradford and Wakefield, and was also close to the point where many expresses left the company's metals to continue over the Great Northern into Leeds. The Lancashire & Yorkshire lost the opportunity of reaching this city in its own right.

During the latter part of the 19th century the company reformed itself and became quite respectable. By this time it had built the now defunct branches to Rishworth, Stainland and Dewsbury as well as those in the Huddersfield area described in the preceding section. It had gained access to Barnsley and had long established itself as a port-to-port system stretching from Liverpool to Goole via Manchester, the Calder Valley main line, Wakefield and Pontefract. As an east - west route it tended to play second string to the former London & North Western line once the Grouping had taken effect, and the decline gradually continued, to culminate in 1970 in the withdrawal of the through York - Manchester trains.

Opposite: Sowerby Bridge in the 1950s before modernisation swept away much of the railway and the town. A WD 2-8-0 is trundling past on a coal train,

C.W.S.
C.W.S.
C.W.S.

Mytholmroyd station, seen here about 1900, looks fairly conventional from platform level, but in fact is perched on the steeply sloping valley side and the buildings on the left are three storeys above the roadway.

A York - Manchester dining car express near Mytholmroyd in pre-Grouping days headed by "Atlantic" No. 1424. Much of the Calder Valley main line had been quadrupled by 1906, but on certain sections the harsh topography prevented such work being put in hand.

The Lancashire & Yorkshire made a pioneer attempt in 1907 to combat tramcar competition by introducing steam rail-motors on its branches from Greetland to Stainland and Sowerby Bridge to Rishworth. One such train, with an additional trailer coach, is shown at West Vale station on the Stainland branch about 1926.

On both branches new rail-level halts were opened as an additional inducement to passengers. Here rail-motor No. 1, with original coach, is pausing at Watson's Crossing Halt on the Rishworth branch. The rail-motors did not achieve a long-term success, and both branches lost their passenger services in 1929.

Copley tunnel on the direct line from Halifax to Sowerby Bridge opened in 1852. A Lancashire & Yorkshire "Atlantic" is emerging from the tunnel portal.

Pomp and circumstance military style at Halifax station with unrebuilt "Scot" No. 6145 as the centrepiece. It was being renamed, losing the prosaic **Condor** and becoming **The Duke of Wellington's Regiment (West Riding)**.

The West Riding railway scene personified at North Bridge station on the **Halifax & Ovenden Junction** railway, jointly owned by the Great Northern and Lancashire & Yorkshire companies. The four-wheeled carts, general down-at-heel appearance and the poster advertising "funerals completely furnished" all contribute to the period flavour.

Wyke & Norwood Green on the Halifax - Bradford line had its main buildings on the roadway above the station. This view, dating from about 1925, is looking north towards the 1,365 yards Wyke tunnel.

The Lancashire & Yorkshire's finest terminus in the West Riding was Bradford (Exchange) with its double-arched roof. 4-4-2 No. 1407 prepares to depart alongside a train of Great Northern six-wheelers. By the 1960s the condition of the roof was causing serious concern, and in 1973 the station was closed to be replaced by a smaller terminus forming part of a new transport interchange.

One of the major stations in the area which has been completely obliterated is Low Moor, in steam days the point where Leeds (Central) - Manchester services would combine with a portion from Bradford (Exchange). The introduction of diesel units in 1962 made it practical for these services to serve Bradford en route by means of reversal at Exchange, and thus Low Moor lost its main reason for existence and closed only three years later.

Another junction now shorn of most of its former glory is Mirfield, like Low Moor once infamous as a point where passengers were becalmed awaiting desultory connections. The company, as if proud of its lamentable time-keeping, provided a billiards saloon on the station to help while away the passing hours! This view is looking east from the station with a coal train passing an unusually quiet locomotive shed.

A pre-Grouping study of Darton station on the Horbury - Barnsley (Exchange) line, looking north towards Wakefield. This route was promoted in 1846 with the extraordinarily long title of the Sheffield, Rotherham, Barnsley, Wakefield, Huddersfield & Goole Railway, and was opened in 1850.

Several changes had taken place at Darton by 1955 when this Wakefield - Barnsley local paused at the station. The oil lamps had been superseded by gas and the signal box moved on to the platform, but stone setts were still in evidence.

Coal on the move as 0-8-0 No. 79 storms along the Calder Valley main line at Horbury. The first four wagons in this evocative photograph are private owner trucks, part of a vast fleet which once added much colour and interest to freight trains.

In the 1830s and early 1840s the then new-tangled railways were a subject of fascination to many artists, and numerous lithographs and prints were executed. This study of Wakefield (Kirkgate) appeared in ''Views on the Manchester & Leeds Railway'' by A.F. Tait, published in 1845.

The Wakefield, Pontefract &
Goole Railway, absorbed by
the Lancashire & Yorkshire in
1847, was notable for the
over-decorated nature of
many of its stations. This
trend is clearly shown at
Featherstone, between
Wakefield and Pontefract,
with the elaborate gables and
roof arrangement.

Norton, on the line from
Pontefract to Doncaster,
displays ostentatiousness to
the point of absurdity. The
station was closed in 1947 but
is still in use as a private
residence.

East from Woodhead

Woodhead, chronologically the second of the great trans-Pennine tunnels, has a fame and notoriety far exceeding those of its neighbours which to most non railway enthusiasts are but names on a map. One reason is its isolated and windswept location, over a thousand feet above sea level on the summit reaches of what was originally the Sheffield, Ashton-under-Lyne & Manchester Railway. Another is that no less than 26 navvies were killed and 140 injured during its construction, in many cases allegedly due to intoxication, creating such a public outcry that Parliament was compelled to take action. Opened in 1845 and described as "a wondrous triumph of art over nature", the 3 miles 22 yards single line tunnel was like both Summit and Standedge the longest in Britain at the time of its completion.

By the time a second tunnel was opened in 1852 the original company had merged with other systems to form the Manchester, Sheffield & Lincolnshire Railway stretching eastwards to an important North Sea outlet at Grimsby. Major developments occurred in the 1860s with the absorption of the homespun and highly idiosyncratic South Yorkshire Railway, promoted by local coal owners to link Barnsley with Sheffield and Doncaster. This was developed and extended so that by the end of the decade the company possessed a cross-country route from Manchester to Thorne, from where running powers over the North Eastern gave it access to Goole and Hull. The Manchester, Sheffield & Lincolnshire became a close rival to the Midland throughout South Yorkshire, although many of its shareholders remained unimpressed and averred that its initials stood for "Money Sunk and Lost". They were even more alarmed when in 1897 the company changed its name to the Great Central Railway, and far too late in the day built an enormously expensive extension through the Midlands to London (Marylebone). It was soon realised there was not enough traffic to support a fourth trunk route from the metropolis to the north, and so the new initials now meant "Gone Completely".

The mainstay and in many ways the most spectacular part of Great Central operations remained the haulage of "black diamonds", whether eastwards to its coal port at Immingham or over the Pennines to Lancashire. In 1905 new marshalling yards worked by purpose-built locomotives were constructed at Wath-on-Dearne in the heart of the South Yorkshire coalfield to facilitate this traffic. From here strings of westbound coal trains would toil up the long climb to Woodhead, including the vicious 1 in 40 Worsborough bank, creating impressive sound effects and taking about $2\frac{1}{4}$ hours to cover the 19 miles. Matters were slightly eased in 1925 when the LNER built Europe's most powerful steam locomotive, a 2-8-8-2 Beyer Garratt, specially for banking these 850 ton trains, but it was not until 1952 that the problem was largely overcome when 1,500 volt d.c. overhead electrification was instituted between Wath and Dunford Bridge. Two years later this was extended to both Manchester and Sheffield, the work involving the construction of a completely new tunnel at Woodhead, and passenger traffic between the two cities increased by 37 per cent in six weeks. In 1970, however, all through passenger workings were diverted to the Midland's Hope Valley route through Derbyshire, enabling Sheffield (Victoria) station to be closed.

The best known of the tunnels on the trans-Pennine routes has always been Woodhead, and photographs of the imposing western portals are legion. The Dunford Bridge end of the tunnel has received less attention, perhaps because it is almost concealed by a vertical-sided cutting. Ex Great Central 2-8-0 No! 6276 is rumbling east on a long freight — a scene that vanished in 1954 when the route was electrified.

Dunford Bridge station, almost a thousand feet above sea level and the highest in the West Riding apart from those on the Settle - Carlisle line. Note the vast water tank dominating the up platform and the activity at the goods wharf in the background with stone flags awaiting dispatch.

Penistone station about 1903, with class 2A 4-4-0 No. 689 on an up local train of six-wheeled stock. The bogie coaches in the right background are standing on the Huddersfield line.

Wortley station, between Penistone and Deepcar, about 1905. It was closed to passengers in 1955, but this portion of the ex Great Central main line is still traversed by a Sheffield - Huddersfield service.

Much smoke and bustle at Sheffield (Victoria) in early LNER days. The passenger lift giving direct access to the street below for a fare of one penny is of particular interest.

Sheffield (Victoria) about 1898 with class 2 4-4-0 No. 700 on the centre road.
At the time of its opening in 1851, a contemporary description referred to "this costly station covered with a light glass roof like that of the Crystal Palace".

In 1954 the whole concept of Manchester - Sheffield working changed with electrification of the route and completion of the new Woodhead tunnel. CoCo No. 27005 "Minerva" pauses at Penistone on an up train in May 1960. Ten years later these services were withdrawn and replaced by diesel-hauled trains on the Midland's Hope Valley route, enabling Sheffield (Victoria) station to be closed.

Silkstone station on the Penistone - Barnsley line, served by a local service between Penistone and Doncaster until its withdrawal in 1959. The rather drab brick building typifies West Riding railway architecture.

Barnsley (Court House) station on a June evening in 1947. LMS 0-4-4T No. 1368 has just arrived on a local from Sheffield (Midland), while LNER 4-4-2T No. 7411 is awaiting departure for Penistone. An interior view of Court House station is shown on page 14.

Two closely parallel routes competed for traffic between Sheffield and Barnsley until 1953 when passenger services on the older established Great Central line were withdrawn. Some sections of this route were surprisingly attractive as shown in the wooded background to this study of 4-4-2T No. 67409 at Chapeltown.

Ex Great Central locomotives at Barnsley locomotive depot, hard by the then single platform of Exchange station. Once referred to as "a disgraceful and beastly hole", the station's facilities were improved when the engine sheds were demolished and a second platform erected in their place.

Wombwell, a large station on the Barnsley-Mexborough-Doncaster line, which replaced an earlier structure in 1877. Coal trains heading west from the South Yorkshire coalfield to Lancashire have always formed the principal traffic on this now electrified line.

The impressive track layout at Stainforth & Hatfield station in its heyday with much freight traffic in evidence. The Doncaster-Hull line was joined here by the West Riding & Grimsby route from Wakefield.

A familiar scene from the steam age as a goods train pauses to take water at Doncaster. The locomotive is double-framed 0-6-0 No. 462, as modified by Robinson.

South Yorkshire Mineral Lines

By no means all the vast amount of coal traffic stemming from South Yorkshire was the exclusive preserve of the Midland and Great Central companies. As technological developments caused collieries to spread eastwards from Barnsley to Doncaster from the 1880s onwards, so new companies sprang up with an eye to catching the additional traffic. The first of these was promoted in 1880 as the Hull, Barnsley & West Riding Junction Railway & Dock (it mercifully shortened its title to the Hull & Barnsley in 1905), and was an attempt to break the monopoly held by the North Eastern Railway over the export of coal traffic through Hull. It took the form of a reasonably direct main line from the coalfield to the company's own dock at Hull, but despite its name never reached Barnsley and was often unkindly referred to as "petering out among the spoil heaps west of Cudworth". Even though it ran across relatively easy terrain, the Hull & Barnsley cost £60,000 per mile — largely owing to lax management — and was the most expensive railway of any substantial length to be built in Britain. It drifted deeper and deeper into debt, only moving towards solvency when it patched up a working arrangement with its arch rival — the North Eastern — so that co-operation replaced futile competition. Although primarily a mineral line, the company operated a number of passenger services including some expresses between Hull and Sheffield (Midland).

The Hull & Barnsley took over two nominally independent concerns which gave it access to Wath-on-Dearne, Denaby and the intervening coalfield to the north. This region was also penetrated by the Dearne Valley Railway, completed in 1909 as an off-shoot of the Lancashire & Yorkshire Railway and extending south-east from near Wakefield to Black Carr junction on the Great Northern main line south of Doncaster. Almost lost in the industrial landscape for most of its length, it had a fleeting stretch of structural glory in the shape of the 113 feet high Conisbrough viaduct taking the line high across the river Don and immediately followed by a 70 feet deep cutting through gleaming white magnesian limestone. A passenger service was operated from Wakefield to Edlington, near Conisbrough, mainly to cater for the needs of colliery workers.

Even the Dearne Valley was not the end of the story for quite a network of lines was built to serve new "super pits" which mushroomed in hitherto most attractive countryside between Worksop and Mexborough. Completed in 1916, these lines heralded a new era in that they were built on a joint rather than a competitive basis and — with the exception of the London & North Western — involved all of the major companies with an interest in the West Riding. Substantial portions of this joint network still survive, as does much of the Dearne Valley system, but the Hull & Barnsley has effectively been wiped off the map. It lost its West Riding passenger services as early as 1932, and its demise was virtually complete when through mineral workings ceased in 1958.

The Hull & Barnsley Railway had, in addition to its main line, a number of important feeder routes. One of these was the South Yorkshire Junction Railway, extending from Wrangbrook junction to Denaby, which it worked from the outset. Here 0-6-2T No. 104 pauses at the intermediate station of Sprotborough.

The Dearne Valley Railway was a relatively insignificant line trailing through the coalfield, but nevertheless boasted the magnificent Conisbrough viaduct with its 21 arches and 150 feet wide central span at a height of 113 feet above the river Don. The line across it was abandoned in 1966.

The Hull & Barnsley Railway never actually reached Barnsley, and was often unkindly referred to as "Petering out among the spoil heaps west of Cudworth". Yet its eight-road locomotive depot at Cudworth showed that the company meant business. In this photograph from the early LNER period all the engines are ex Hull & Barnsley classes.

In complete contrast was the tiny shed at Denaby, the terminus of the South Yorkshire Junction line. 0-6-2T No. 2487 is poking its nose out of the shed in June 1925.

Some of the South Yorkshire mineral lines did also have a meagre passenger service. The Great Central Railway operated passenger trains over the South Yorkshire Joint line from Doncaster to Shireoaks (later Worksop) from 1910 until 1929. Here an inaugural inspection train pauses at Tickhill & Wadworth station in September 1908 prior to the commencement of regular services.

The Dearne Valley Railway decided to cater for passenger traffic in 1912, and built some superbly economical stations — rail-level platforms with an old carriage as a waiting room! The dominant structure in this 1933 view of Denaby is the nameboard. A service between Wakefield and Edlington was operated by rail-motors and then push-and-pull trains until its withdrawal in 1951.

Acknowledgements

The photographs have been supplied by the following individuals and collections. Figures relate to page numbers; B=bottom; T=top:

H. C. Casserley and collection: 11T, 17B, 27T, 32T, 47T, 48T, 58T, 67, 70B, 74, 78, 79B.

W. A. Camwell: 14B, 23B, 31B, 33B, 38T, 39T, 62B, 72B, 73T.

J. B. Hodgson collection: 25, 48B, 56B, 57, 60T, 61B, 65T, 77B.

David Joy and collection: 15B, 18, 19, 21B, 24T, 33T, 36T, 56T, 64.

Eric Treacy: Front and back covers, 35, 43, 55.

Locomotive & General Railway Photographs: 16, 17T, 21T, 60B, 63, 73B.

Biltcliffe collection: 68, 69, 70T, 72T.

British Railways: 12, 20, 50.

Rixon Bucknall collection: 37T, 51B, 71T, 77T.

J. E. Kite collection: 27B, 38B, 40B, 62T.

Real Photographs Co.: 23T, 28, 45, 46.

Gordon Biddle: 31T, 32B, 65B.

Yorkshire Post Newspapers: 34, 37B, 52T, 53T.

Halifax Courier: 58B, 59.

D. Ibbotson: 47B, 49T.

Locomotive Club of Great Britain (Ken Nunn collection): 14T, 75.

John Marshall and collection: 36B, 51T, 71B.

Sheffield City Libraries: 9, 10.

Oliver Carter: 13.

R. M. Casserley: 49B.

J. M. Crowther: 44B.

J. K. Ellwood collection: 24B.

W. Hubert Foster: 22B.

Fox Photos: 30.

Alan R. Hainsworth collection: 39B.

K. Hoole collection: 44T, 53B.

Leeds City Libraries: 52B.

Edgar W. Morrell: 41.

Photomatic: 29.

R. F. Roberts: 11B.

F. W. Smith: 22T.

South Yorkshire Industrial Museum: 79T.

S. Sutcliffe collection: 40T.

J. F. Thomas: 61T.

B. W. Wright: 15T.

The map on page 4 is reproduced from the compiler's "A Regional History of the Railways of Great Britain: Vol. 8 South and West Yorkshire" published by David & Charles.